e, u would enjoy
this because you are a-MAZE-ing!
Happy Birthday!
Love, D.

WELCOME TO LABYRINTH:
THE ULTIMATE MAZE BOOK

With 14 worlds to explore, the mazes at the beginning of this book are
created for the youngest detectives. As you work your way through every
page, you'll encounter worlds that are more and more challenging...
and in some cases, only safe for the hardiest explorer.

Choose your own adventure today!

WIDE EYED EDITIONS

Race through the kaleidoscopic crowd to catch the yellow car. On your way, try to spot: a smiling crocodile;

a happy lion; a giant teddy with its pet dog; two shy black cats, and a great big grumpy bug.

Make your way through the magical mansion to deliver the present at the birthday party. On your way, look out for:

a pastry chef baking cookies; a diplodocus by a volcano; a bus stop; a flying magic carpet, and an astronaut.

Guide a monster on the run to find his way home. In the crowds, can you spot: a hairy giant wearing a watch;

a worm with a bowler hat; a glum, stripy bee; a girl holding her teddy, and a cross frog?

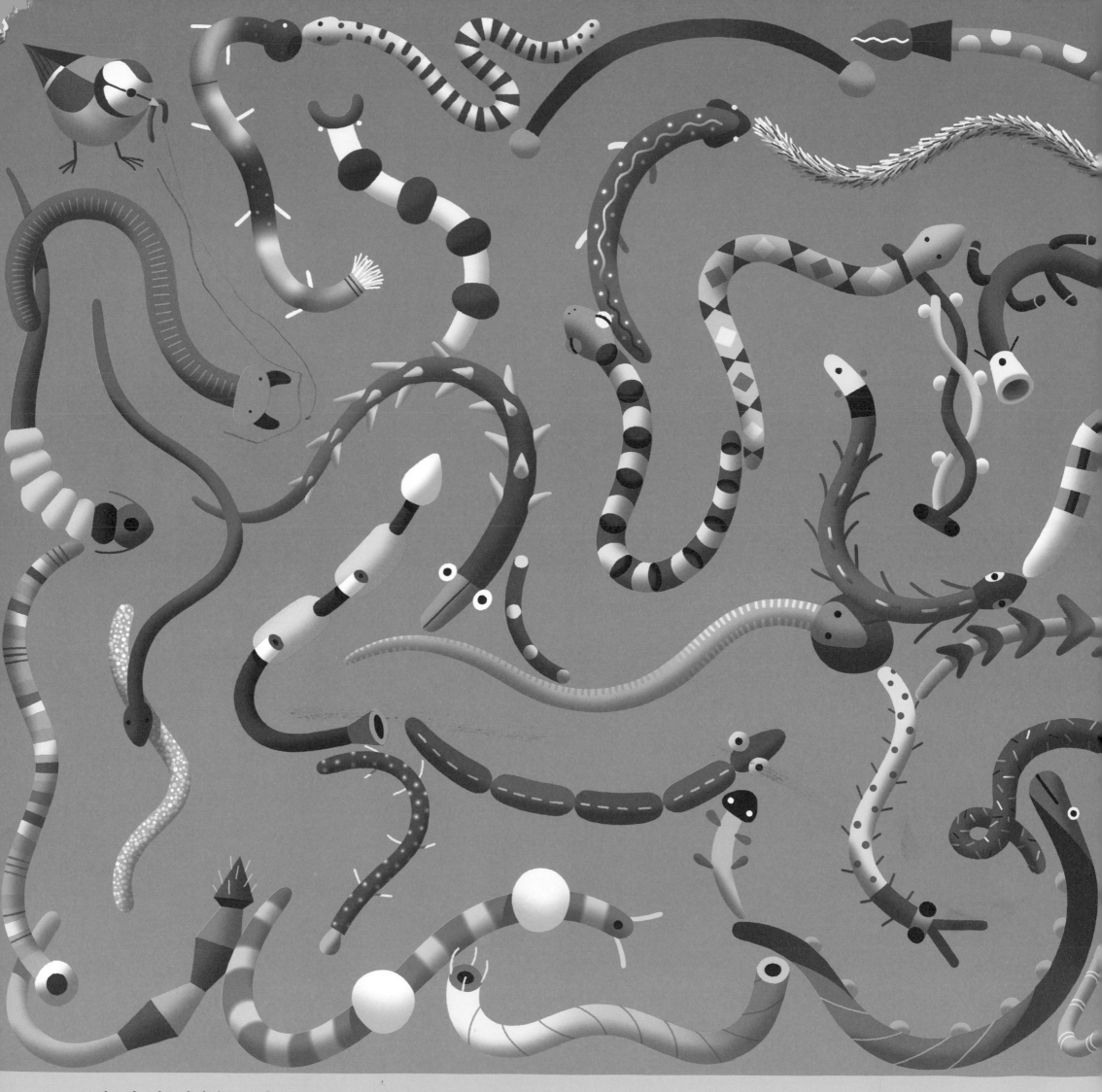

Help the bird deliver the worm to her chicks. On the way, can you spot: a hairy one-eyed worm; a headless, green,

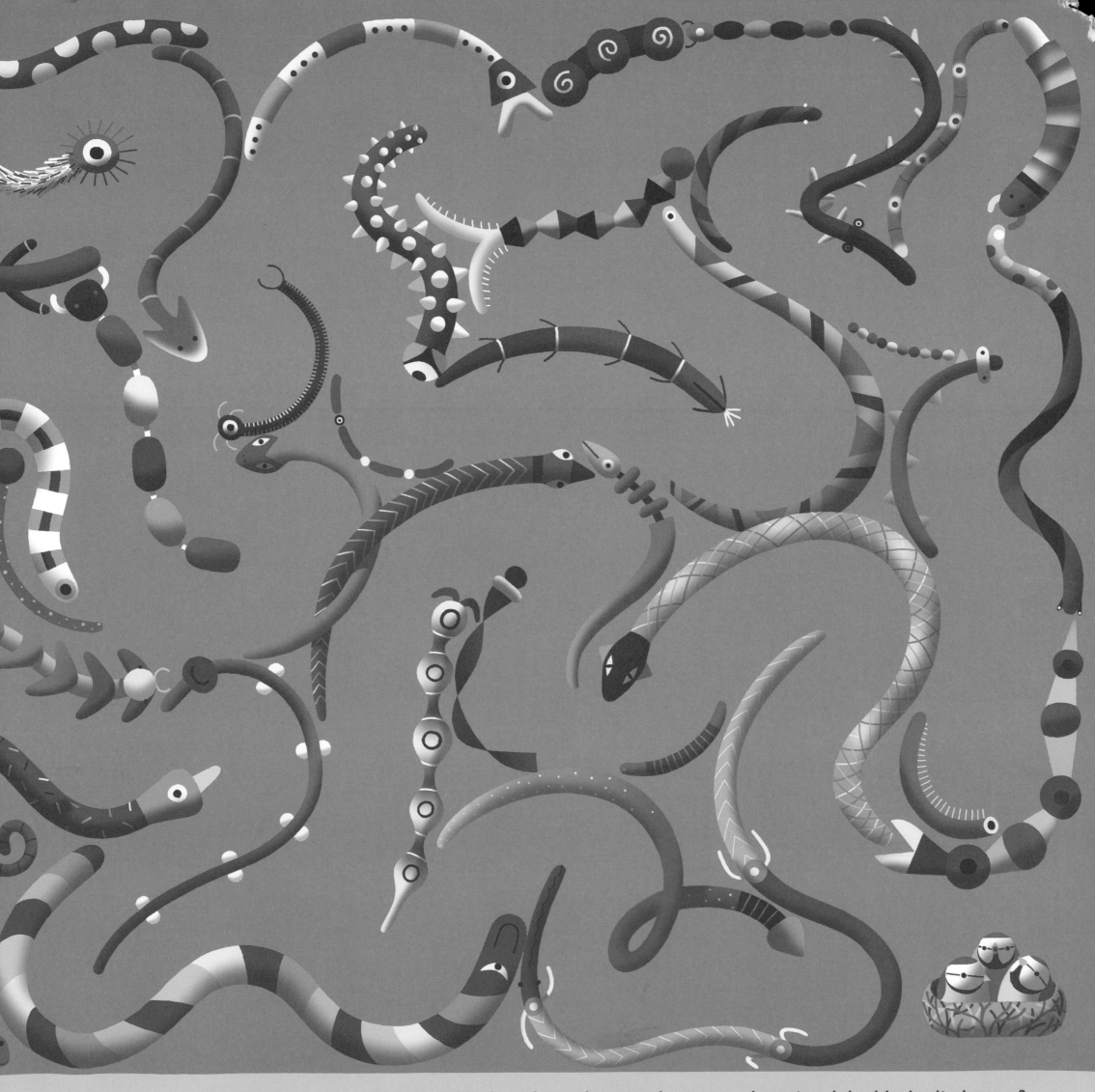

freckly worm; a small, brown, spiraled worm; a black-and-purple striped worm; and a twisted double-bodied worm?

Make a path through the dragon's lair and join the game at the other end. On the way, look out for: a statue

of a sitting boar; a sculpture in a lily pond; a row of four figurines; a cool pool of water, and a statue of a Roman guard.

Show the scuba diver the way through the deep, dark waters, back to his submarine.

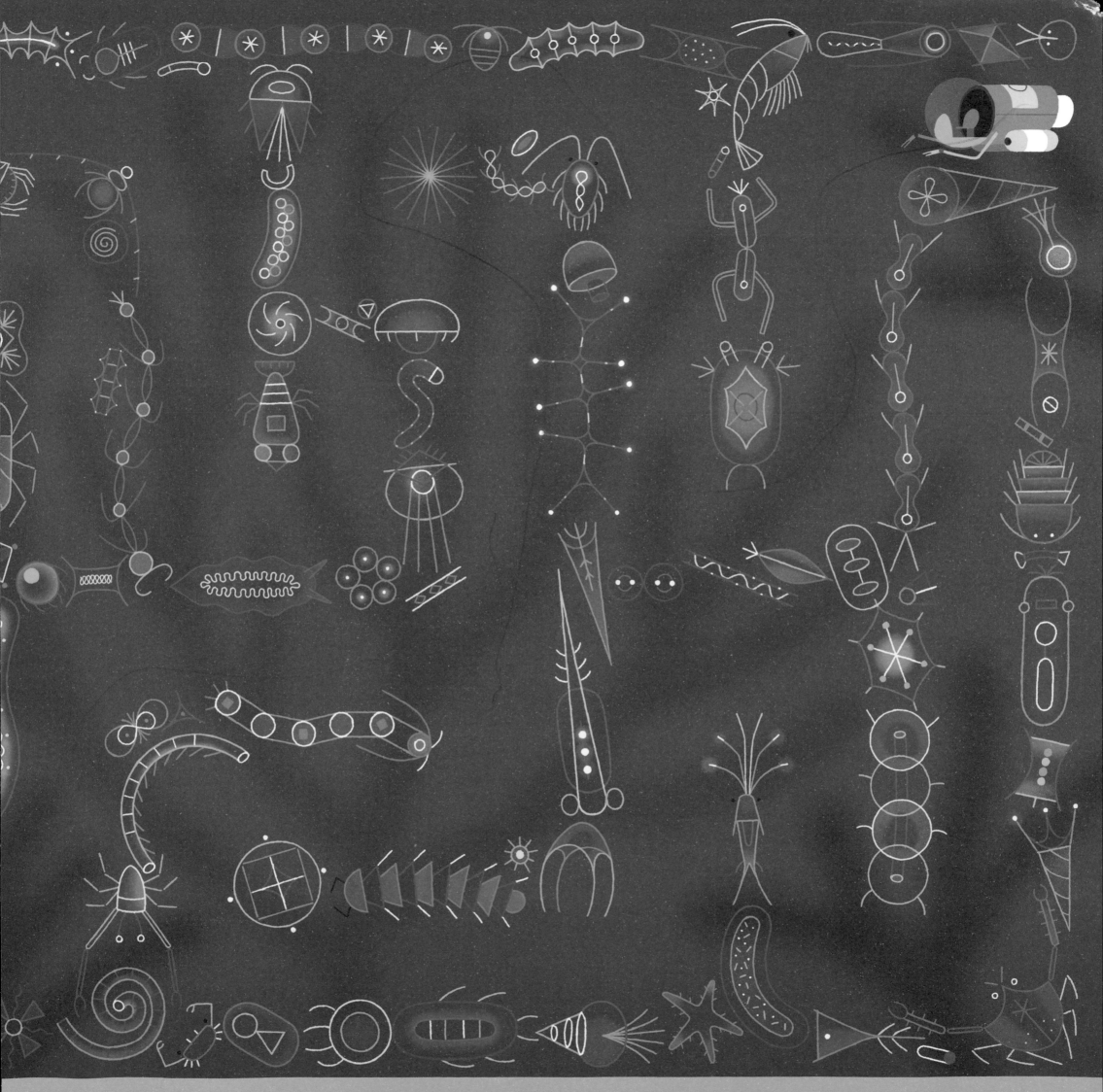

On the way, look out for: a blue crab; a yellow crab; a red crab; a pink starfish, and a yellow shrimp.

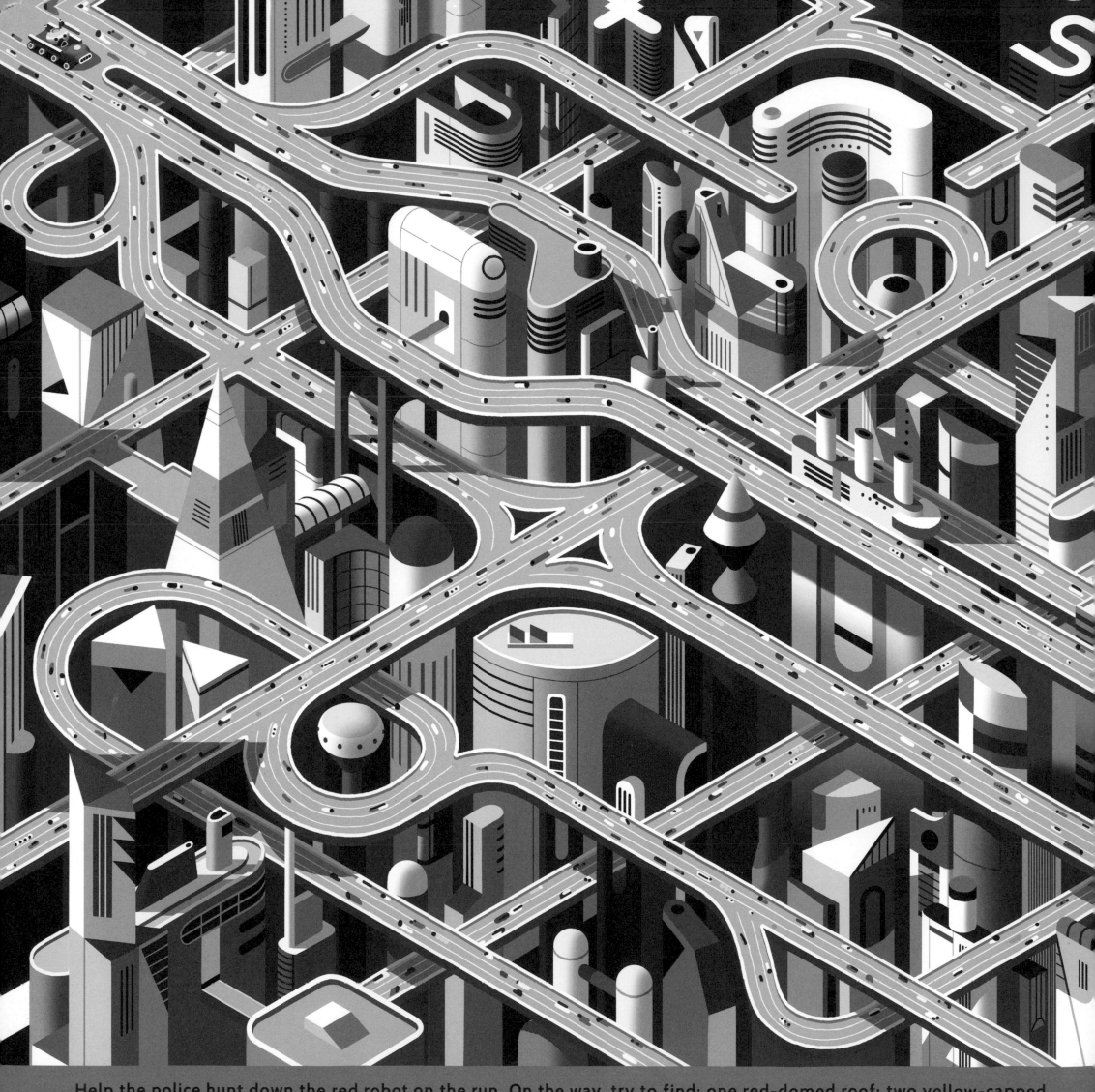

Help the police hunt down the red robot on the run. On the way, try to find: one red-domed roof; two yellow-capped

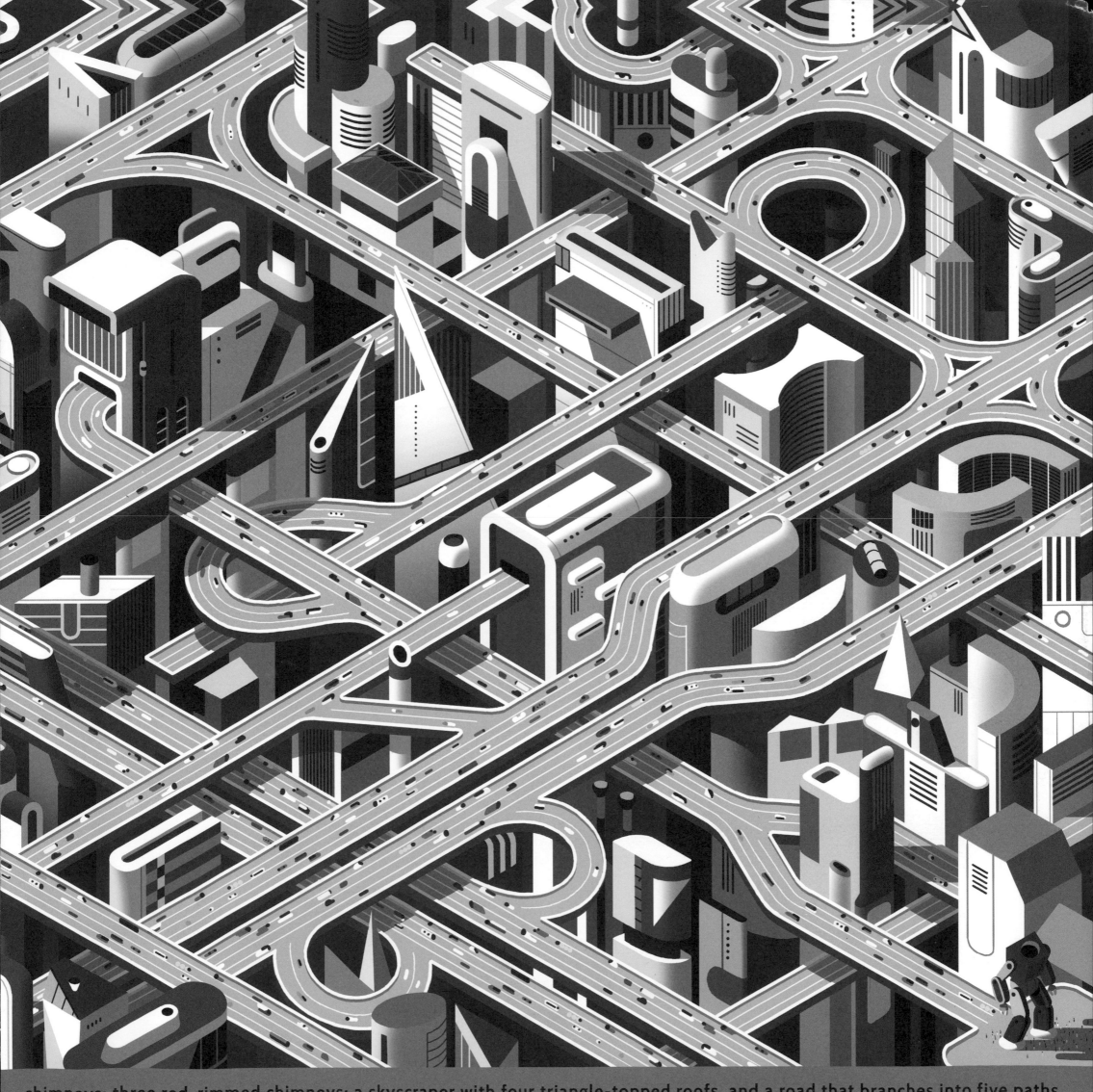

chimneys; three red-rimmed chimneys; a skyscraper with four triangle-topped roofs, and a road that branches into five paths.

The king has laid down the red carpet for his royal guest. Can you find the way to his throne? On the way, look out for: someone

looking out of a window; a roof with a crescent shape; a clock tower; a lady in a violet dress, and two pairs of sentries on guard.

Help the boy find his way to the water. On the way, see if you can spot: a blue towel with bananas on it;

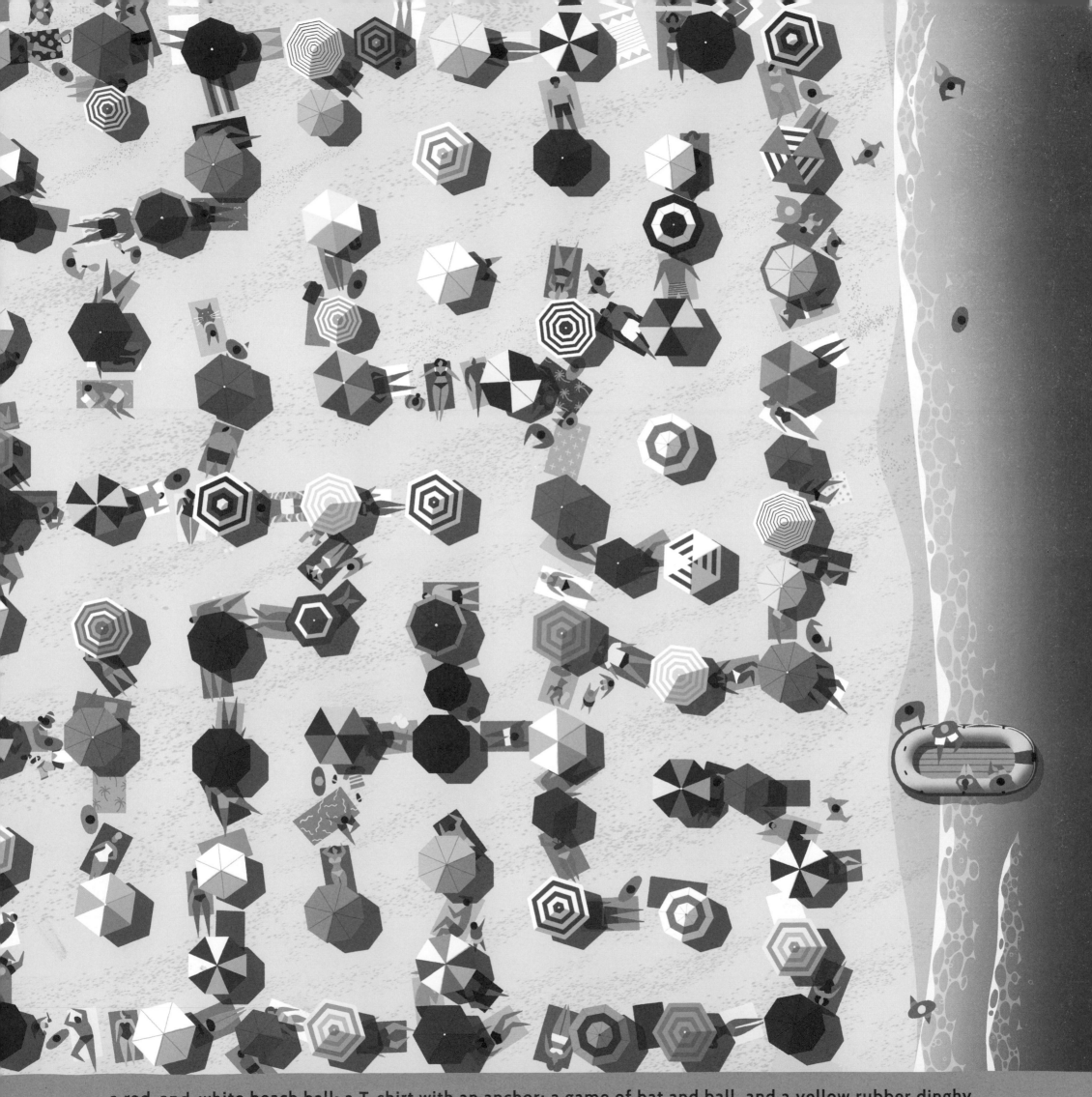

a red-and-white beach ball; a T-shirt with an anchor; a game of bat and ball, and a yellow rubber dinghy.

Quick! Help this young man get to his date! On the way, look out for: one red triangle; a pair of red pipes;

a row of three plants; a group of four art lovers, and five visitors sitting down in different spots.

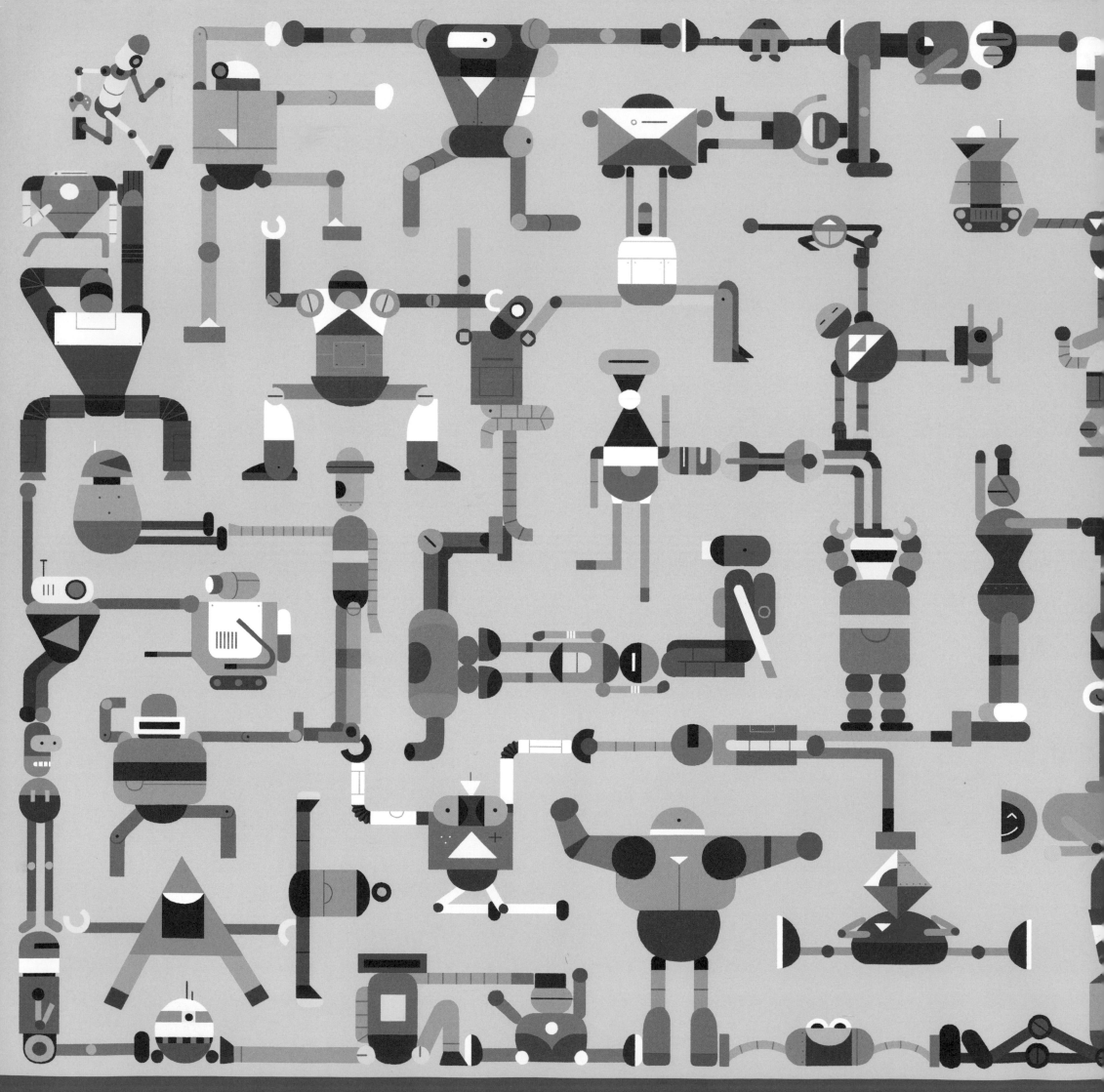

Help the robot get to the game. On the way, can you find: a robot with four fingers and a thumb; a robot with red shoes;

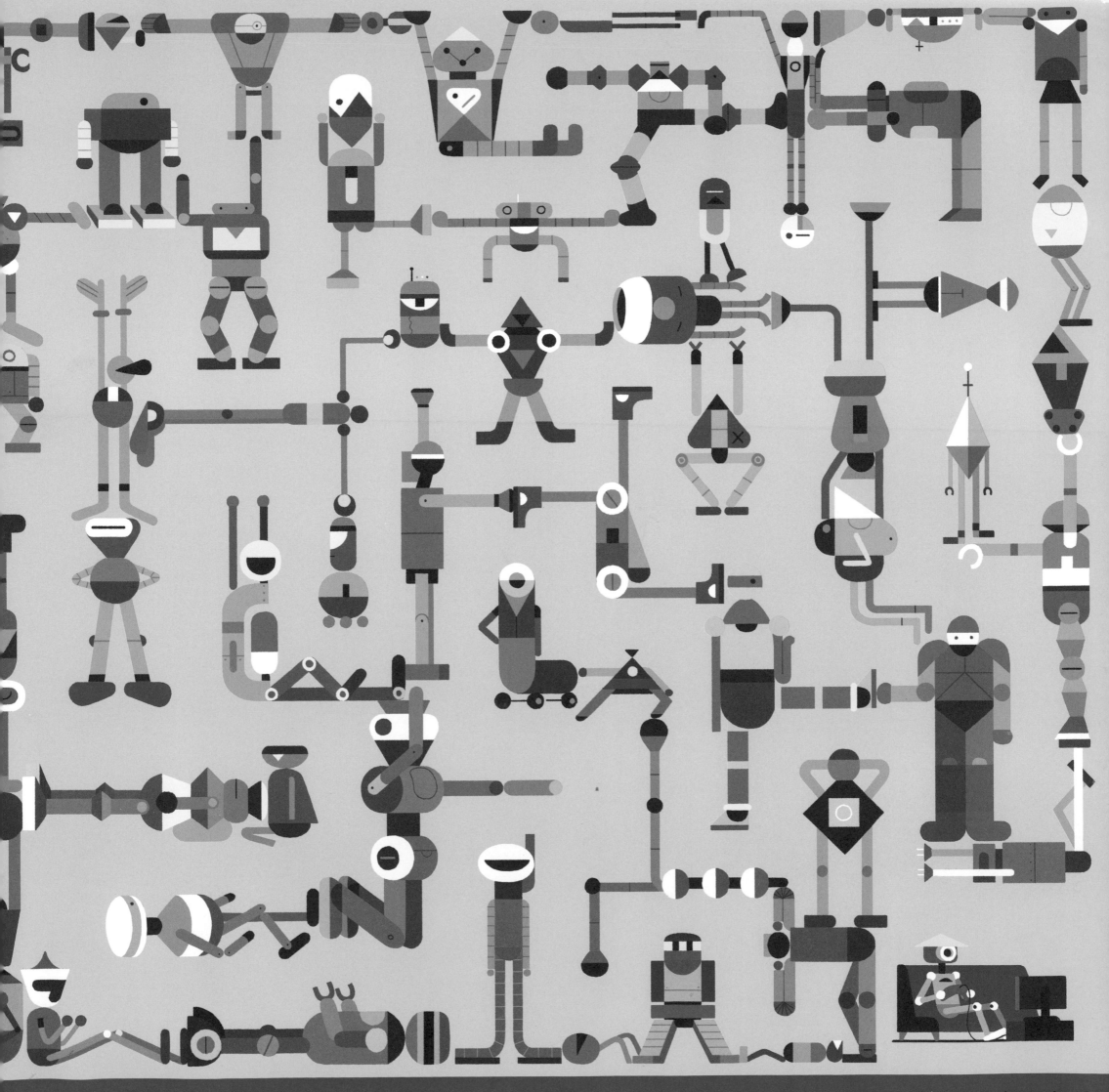

a robot with a green, diamond-shaped body; a robot doing a handstand with his eyes closed, and a robot hanging from the ceiling?

Help the knight discover the treasure. On the way, can you spot: one white square in a purple circle; two white circles on blue

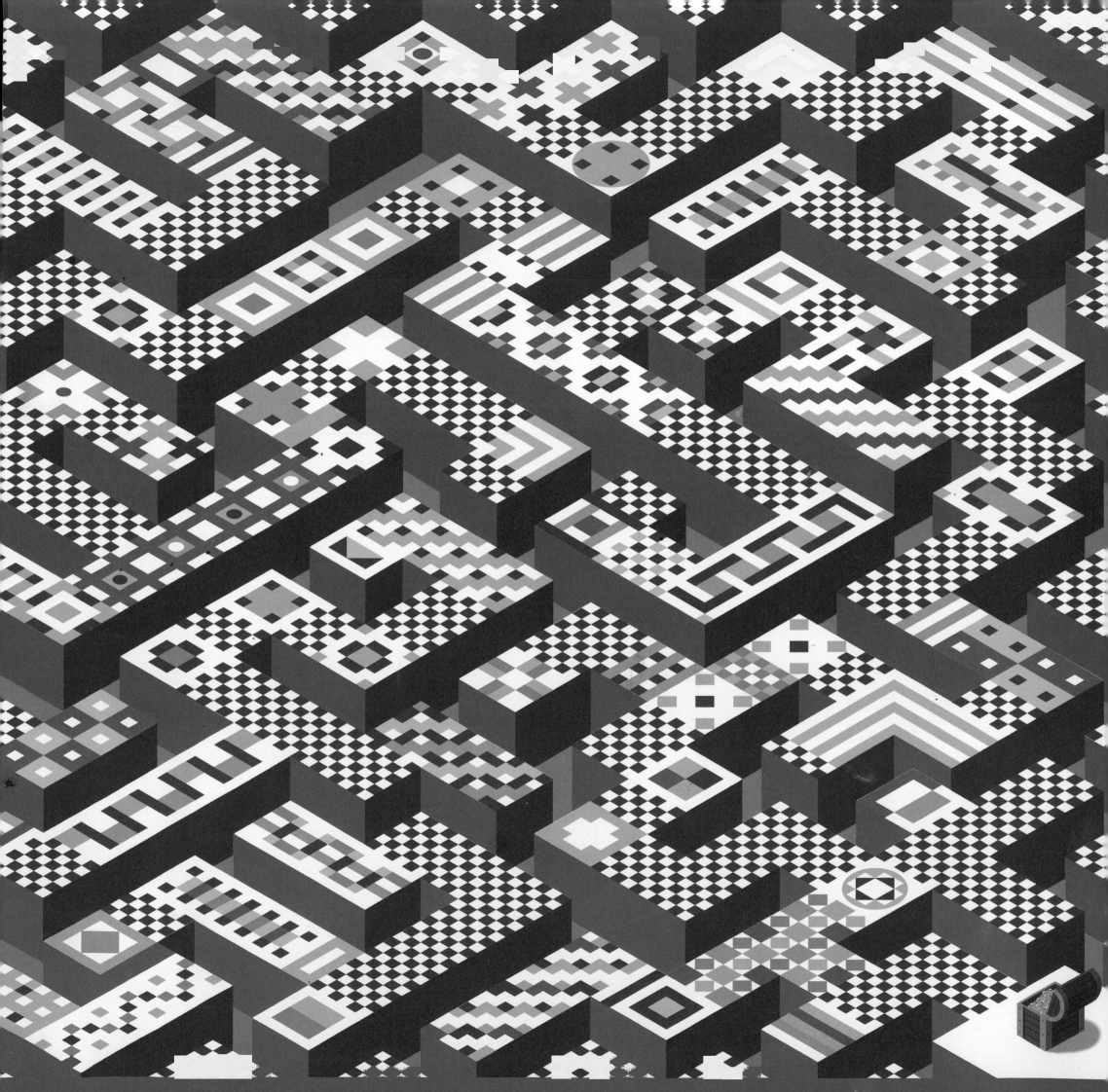

squares; a group of three bending purple lines; four black squares inside a purple circle, and five pairs of black-and-white lines?

Summer is here... but the beach is far away! Help the drivers find their way through town. On the way, can you spot:

a hosepipe; a group playing ball; a clock tower; a blue mailbox, and a boy in a striped top sitting on the grass?

Can you help Square find his way back to his friends? On the way, look out for: one red crescent; two yellow circles

connected by a yellow line; three blue crosses in a row; a block with four pairs of leaves, and five blue lines on an orange block.

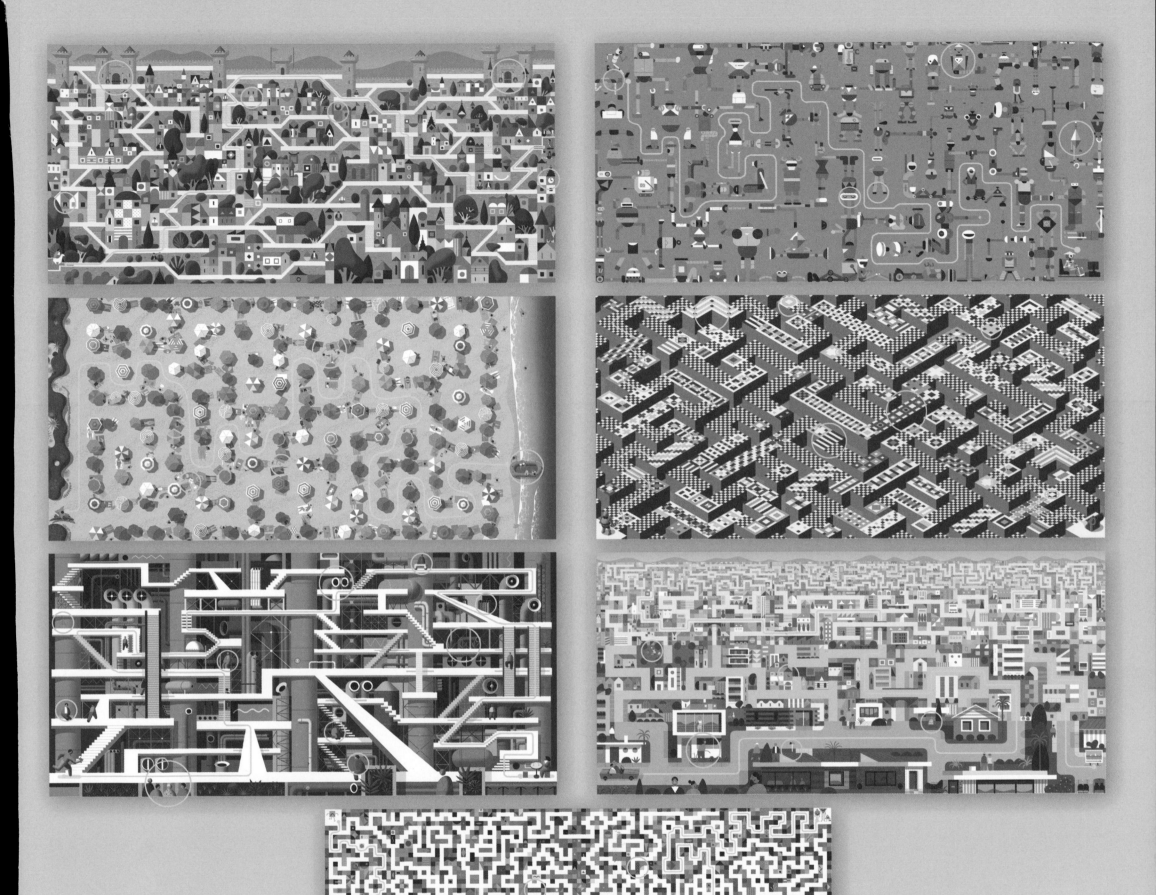

Text and illustration © Théo Guignard 2016

This edition first published in 2017 by
Wide Eyed Editions, an imprint of Aurum Press,
The Old Brewery, 6 Blundell Street, London, N7 9B, UK

Labyrinthes by Théo Guignard first published by Éditions Amaterra in France

QuartoKnows.com
Visit our blogs at QuartoKnows.com

A catalogue record for this book is available
from the British Library.

ISBN 978-1-84780-998-8

The artworks were drawn digitally
Set in Aller Light

Designed by Nicola Price
Edited by Jenny Broom
Published by Rachel Williams

Manufactured in Dongguan, China TL082017

5 7 9 8 6 4